Zikr-e-Lamhat

The Silent Story of a Moment

Raghav Sharma

Dedication

Preface

In the quiet corners of our lives, moments often go unnoticed, like whispers carried away by the wind. *Zikr-e-Lamhat - The Silent Story of a Moment* is an exploration of these fleeting instants, a journey through the tapestry of emotions, memories, and reflections that shape our existence.

Inspired by the beauty of everyday life, I learned to appreciate the profound stories hidden within the ordinary. Through this collection, I aim to share my interpretations of life's delicate moments, drawing from personal experiences, dreams, and the world around me.

Each poem serves as a window into my thoughts, a gentle reminder that every second holds a narrative waiting to be told. As you read, I invite you to pause, reflect, and perhaps discover the silent stories woven into your own life.

This book is not just a collection of poems; it is a tribute to the moments that define us, the emotions that bind us, and the observations that inspire us. I hope that within these pages, you find echoes of your own experiences and a sense of connection to the universal journey we all share.

Thank you for joining me on this voyage through words, where every moment is worthy of remembrance.

Acknowledgements

I want to express my heartfelt gratitude to my late-night friends, whose ears were always open and whose hearts were always warm. Thank you for listening to my thoughts and dreams during those quiet hours. Your support and understanding have inspired me to explore my creativity and share my voice through poetry.

To my family, your unwavering love and encouragement have been my foundation throughout this journey. Your belief in me has given me the strength to pursue my passion for writing with courage and conviction.

I also want to acknowledge the countless individuals who have encouraged me along the way. Your kind words and support have fueled my determination to bring these poems to life. Each of you has played a vital role in this journey, and I am profoundly grateful for your presence in my life.

Lastly, though he may not know it, I owe a debt of gratitude to Gulzar Sahab. His words have inspired countless hearts, including mine, showing us the beauty of observation and the power of poetry.

This collection is a testament to the love and support that surrounds me, and I cherish each of you for being part of this journey.

1. अलविदा

याद है वो दिन जब हम मिले थे हम आखिरी बार..
तुम अलविदा कह कर चली गयी

मैं कुछ देर और तुम्हारे साथ खड़ा रहा।।

GoodBye!

I remember the day we met for the last,
You said goodbye, and slowly walked past.
But I stood with you, though the moment had passed..

2. जवानी

बड़ा उदास सा है जवानी का मौसम,
किसी सर्द रात मै सहमा हुआ सा..

शायद जलता है बचपन की बहार से,
जहाँ ना जाने कब किस महक से मन खुश हो जाता था..

ये दुनिया दारी के ओले,ये ज़िम्मेदारियों कि बारिश,
जितनी अकड़ है उतनी बलवान नहीं है ये जवानी..

बचपन वाली मासूमियत कहा है अब,
मर्ज़ियाँ चाहे पूरी ना हो, निभा लेता था सब..

तब किसी की ज़िम्मेदारी थे आज ज़िम्मेदार हैं,
रोज़ सुबह हर मोड़ पे अब एक चुनौती तयार है..

बचपन में भी जूझ लेते थे अब जवानी की बारी है,
ज़िंदा रहे बचपन सभी मै .. क्योंकि मेरा laptop उसकी किताबो से
भारी है।।

Being Young!

The season of youth is a quiet, sad song,
Like shivering through a cold night, long.
Childhood burned bright from the outside, it seems,
Where simple joys lit the heart in dreams.

This world now hails with storms and rain,
Responsibilities pile, relentless strain.
Youth stands proud, but fragile, too,
Not as strong as it claims to be, we knew.

Where is the innocence we once held tight?
A wish unfulfilled still felt so right.
Back then, others carried our load,
Now, at every turn, another heavy road.

We struggled then, and we struggle still,
But let childhood live in me at will.
For all that's mine, may that part stay,
Guiding me gently through every day.

3. याद

एक याद है तू जो घुली है मिसरी के जैसे
मिठास तेरी हर सांस के आने जाने में है

कुछ बातें हसाती हैं तेरी कुछ रूला जाती है
बस वक़्त की तरह ज़ेहन में चलती जाती हैं

पुरानी बाते जिन्हे कभी मैं बयां करता हूं
तेरी मुस्कुराहट की महक के बिना अधूरी है

अब एक अधूरा सा इश्क एच तेरी यादों से
फिर से जीना चाहता हूँ उन्हें

छेड़ना चाहता हूं रुलाना चाहता हूं हसना चाहता हूं
वो जो पल है उसे घोट के पीना चाहता हूँ

जो कभी खोया उसने नहीं मैंने
उसे अब पाना चाहता हूँ।।

Memory !

A memory of you, dissolved like an ancient dream,
Sweetness lingering in every breath it seems.
Some things bring laughter, some bring tears,
Like time, they drift through the mind for years.

Old stories I tell, but they're never the same,
Without the warmth of your smile, they lose their
flame.
Now love feels incomplete, a shadow of before,
I long to relive those moments once more.

I want to tease, to make you cry, to laugh again,
To drink in the past, to feel its sweet pain.
The part of me that never let go,
Is the one I now seek, the one I want to know..

4. इकतरफा

तमाम पल अब, मेरे हाथ में उसका हाथ होता है
रोज़ सुबह उसकी आंखों का दीदार होता है..

सो जाता हूं तकिए को उसकी गोद समझ कर
इकतरफा प्यार में यूं ही तो होता है।।

One Sided

Every moment now, her hand in mine,
In her eyes, each morning I find a sign.

I drift to sleep, the pillow my embrace,
This is the ache of love, when it's one-sided in space.

5. बारिशें

ये बारिशें दूर घर से बहुत यादें लेके गिरती हैं..
वो यादें जिनका लेखा जोखा भी इन बून्दो जितना ही है..

कुछ यादें जिनका रह-रह एक झोखा आता है..
कुछ यादें जो मिट्टी से नमी चुरा के भर देती हैं आँखों में..

वो यादें जिनके काले बादल आज भी कभी-कभी आँखों में पानी
बरसाते हैं..
वो यादें जिनके बादल धूप रोक कर बचपन की छाँव बचा लेती हैं..

वो यादें जो कड़क के बिजली की तरह एक पल के लिए सहमत होती
हैं..
वो यादें जो लहराते हुए हरे पेड़ो में माँ और कुदरत का फर्क मिटा देती
हैं..

ये यादें ये बारिश सुकून देती हैं जब तक हद में हैं...
हद से आगे खिड़कियाँ बंद कर और यादें रोक के सोना सीख लिया
मैंने।।

Rains

These rains fall far from home, steeped in memories,
As abundant as the drops that dance on trees.

A whiff of the past drifts by now and then,
While some memories, like soil, draw moisture again.

Dark clouds of yore bring tears to the eyes,
Blocking the sunshine, where childhood's shade lies.

They clash like thunder, flicker like lightning,
Blending the comfort of mother and the power of nature,
igniting.

These memories, these rains, bring solace and sighs,
Until the last drop falls and the echo replies.

6. गुमान

ये घर में अकेला मैं
और ये सामान तेरा...

बड़ा भारी पड़ा है मुझे ये गुमान मेरा..

बस अब कभी-कभी खुद से ये बात होती है
मोहब्बत अब मेरी वो है जो बिछड़ने के बाद होती है।।

Pride

I am alone in this house,
Surrounded by things that are yours.
The silence echoes, a heavy cost,
A price my pride silently endures.

I think sometimes, as shadows fall,
That love, the one I now embrace,
Is not the one we used to know—
It blooms in the absence, in empty space.

7. कहकशा

ये रात आईना है मेरी जिंदगी का
ये तारे किस्से हैं मेरे

कुछ टाइम्टिमेट हैं कुछ टूट जाते हैं
बस मुझे ये याद दिलाते हैं..

ये रात दिन के बाद फिर आएगी
ये तारों की चादर फिर लाएगी

दिन उम्मीदों से भरा होगा
कहकशा का फिर मेरे सिर पर हाथ होग।।

Milky Way

This night mirrors the life I lead,
These stars hold my stories near.
Some shine bright, some fade away,
Each one a memory, drawing me here.

Night will return when day is done,
Bringing back the stars' soft glow.
Day will rise, with hope in its light,
And the Milky Way will watch me grow.

8. नमकीन

तू दूर होकर भी इस तरह मुझे तंग करने लगी थी...
रोज़ सूरज के आते ही रात होने लगी थी...

एक शराब वह थी वो अब छोड़ दी है मैंने
तेरी यादें मेरा जाम नमकीन करने लगी थी।।

Salty

Even from afar, you trouble me still,
Each dawn you turn to night at will.

I gave up drinking, your memories wouldn't stop,
They made my glass salty, drop by drop.

९. पुराना रिश्ता

ये एक पुराना रिश्ता है
इसमें जीत या हार तो नहीं...

कुछ बनेगा, कुछ बिगड़ेगा
इसे संभालने का ज़िम्मा हमारा है सिर्फ तेरा तो नहीं...

कुछ हमारी कहानियों का बोझ लेकर सूरज ढल गया है...
चाँद है ना हमारे पास अँधेरा तो नही।।

Old Ties

This is an old, familiar tie,
No victory, no defeat in sight.
Things will be made, things will fall,
It's ours to mend, not just your fight.

The sun has set with stories to keep,
Carrying burdens we couldn't speak.
But we have the moon, a guiding light,
No darkness now, just soft, calm night.

10. आदत

मैं उसके आने पर बस उसका हो जाऊंगा और वो सुबह तक बस मेरे
ख्वाब सुनेगी..
ये रात से सौदा कर लिया है मैंने

उसे तो नहीं आना है अब ये जानता हूं मैं
बस वो उसकी याद ना आने की आदत बहुत याद आती है।।

Habit

I'll be hers when she returns,
She'll listen to my dreams till dawn.

I've struck this deal with the night,

Knowing it won't bring her along.
I just miss the habit of forgetting her by night.

11. घर

तेरे सिरहाने सिर रख कर सोता था सुकुन में इक घर रख कर..
वो घर जिसका हर पत्थर तेरी गोद की तरह मुझे सुकुन देता था..

हर खिड़की उसकी आंख तेरी बन के प्यार की धूप से भर देती थी मुझे..
छत उसकी तेरी बाहों की तरह बुलाती थी मुझे और जकड़ लेती थी जैसे

अभी-अभी कोई बिजली का लाव आया था..

तू नहीं है अब , नींद नहीं मेरी रात चुरा ली है तूने..
उस घर के बाहर अब रोज़ घड़ी के कांटो में चांद डूबा देता हूं मैं

चला जाता हु रोज सुबह
रात के लिए सूखी यादें लेने।।

House

I used to sleep with my head by yours,
In a house where peace would reign,
Each stone a comfort, like your lap,
A sanctuary from all my pain.
Your eyes filled every window bright,
Sunshine pouring from your love.
The ceiling called me, arms outstretched,
Holding me close, as if from above.
But now an electric flame has sparked,
You're gone, sleep has fled; you've stolen my night.
Each day I place the moon outside,
Setting the clock in fading light.
Each morning, I return once more,
To gather dry memories for the night.

12. हर रात

अब साथ हैं तो आ , एक दूसरे के हो जाएं

यू नज़रो का खेल ना कर

ना हो ऐसा कि हमारी लापरवाही से ये रात चोरी हो जाए

थोड़ी इफ़ाज़त से तो रख तू भी कभी मुझको..

यू ना हो कि फिर से मेरी आंख खुले और सपना टूट जाये।।

Each Night

Now that we're together, let's be side by side,
Don't play with your eyes, don't let love hide.

Lest this night be stolen by careless hearts,
Please show me kindness before it departs.

For if my eyes open, dreams may shatter,
In this fragile moment, let's hold what matters.

13. अफ़्सुरदगी

कुछ ख़ुशियों के पेड़ बोता हूँ जब एक सफ़र पे जाने का सोचता हूँ..

थोड़ा हट के जिम्मेदारियो से,थोड़ा हट के दफ्तर की कशमकश से,
बस खुली आंखो वाला सपना पूरा करता हूं..
निकल जाता हूं कैसे भी मैं अपने अंदर के शहर को चुप कराने, ऐसी
जगह जहां सुकून का शोर होता है..

किस्मत कुछ यू हाथ फेरती है सर पर मेरे, कुछ यूं मैं खुश हो जाता
हूं... जब कुछ अपने जैसे अंजानों से बरसों का साथ महसूस होता है..

वो मेरा शहर जहां मुझे सब जानते हैं, वाह की चमक मेरे अँधेरे भर
नहीं पाती, और इस सफर की रातें अंजानों के बीच मुझे रोशन रखती
है...

ये अफ़्सुरदगी में सोचता हूँ क्या इन सब से मिलना लिखा था, या हम
सब अपनी किस्मत की श्याही दूसरे की कोरी किताबों पे लिख के मन
हल्का कर लेते हैं...

एक ख़राब बात है इस सफर की...ये ख़त्म होता है...जब सबसे
मिलकर जाने के बाद वो एक हल्का सा आंसू कहीं होता है...

तब अफ़्सुरदगी में एक एहसास होता है...

ये लोग ये यादें शायद फिर ना हो,

और जो ये शायद है इसी से आगे का हौसला होता है।।

Melancholy

I plant trees of happiness as I dream of a journey,
Escaping the weight of office tasks, where I find my own
yearning.
I leave behind the silent city within, where peace's
whispers reside,
In fate's gentle embrace, I discover joy, a warmth I can't
hide.

Here, strangers like me share the years we've known,
In a city of familiarity, yet the glow can't fill my
darkened tone.
It lights up the nights of this journey, weaving through
unfamiliar faces,
In this melancholy wonder, did we all plan these
embraces?

Or, Did we etch our destinies on each other's blank
pages,
As the journey unfolds, revealing life's fleeting stages?
Yet there's a sorrow woven in this tale's gentle end,

A small tear lingers after giving, as memories begin to
bend.

These faces, these moments, may never cross again,
Yet perhaps this is what fuels our courage to ascend.

14. बोझ

ना जाने कितनी कहानियों का बोझ लेकर ये सूरज ढल जाता है..

बचे हुए दर्द, ख़ुशी, ख़्वाब चाँद के हवाले कर जाता है।।

Burden

Who knows how many stories the setting sun bears,
Carrying the weight of unspoken prayers.
He hands the remaining pain, joy, and dreams,
To the waiting moon, where hope softly gleams.

15. बड़े

बागीचे में वो झूला वक्त का लंगर बन के झूलता है
रोज़ एक लड़का आदमी होने की दौड़ में अपनी सच्चाई कुबूलता है..

कब ना जाने हम भाई बहन एक दूसरे के घर मेहमान हो जाते हैं
अच्छा तो नहीं लेकिन ना चाहते हुए भी 'बड़े' हो जाते है।।

Grown!

That swing in the garden rocks like time's embrace,
Each day a boy faces truth in the manhood race.

Who knows when we siblings become guests in each home?
Though it's bittersweet, we grow up alone.

16. तू मेरा ग़ालिब है...

तू वो ग़ज़ल है, जिसका हर शेर पर खुदा
कि वाह निकलती है!

तू वो जड़ है जिसका पेड़ ना जाने अभी कितने आसमां चीरेगा,

तू मेरा ग़ालिब है...

तेरी हर शायरी मुझे और प्यासा करोड़ देती है,
तू और नज़्मो से मुझे घूँट-घूंट पानी पिलाता है...

रोज़गार से दूर जब कभी दोस्तों के साथ समंदर किनारे जाता हूँ,
उस महफ़िल से किनारा कर के तेरे लफ़्ज़ों के समंदर में सूरज डूबा
देता हूँ...

तू मेरा ग़ालिब है...

जब घर से दूर याद आती है घर की
तो तेरी नज़्मों को घर बना कर इंच दर इंच

अपनी यादें सींचता रहता हूं...

तू चंद लफ़्ज़ों से वक़्त को निचोड़ कर लम्हा कर देता है
मैं जब तेरे साथ होता हूं तो घड़ी नहीं देखता...

तू मेरा ग़ालिब है...

तेरे अल्फ़ाज़ ऐसे खेलते हैं मन में...
जैसे सूरज की किरण में छूटे अंश खेलते हैं...
ना जेन कौन सी स्याही उड़ाता है तू
जो हवा वाह-वाह कहती हुई बहने लगती है...

मोतियों वाला हार सा है वक्त मेरा तूने मुझको पीरो के रखा है...
'गुलज़ार' तू मेरा ग़ालिब है..

My Ghalib!

In closing, I have penned a poem dedicated to Gulzar Sahab inspired by some of his lines, but I have chosen not to translate it. Words often fall short when trying to capture the essence of his artistry. Some sentiments are best expressed in their original form, where the depth and beauty of his influence can truly be felt.

www.ingramcontent.com/pod-product-compliance
Lightning Source LLC
Chambersburg PA
CBHW061729130726
47996CB00006B/2560